Gardens in the Moonlight

What Plants Do at Night

By Margaret Williamson

Discover Plants and Animals
Vowel Teams
(ie, igh)

Scan this code to access the Teacher's Notes for this series or visit
www.norwoodhousepress.com/decodables

NORWOOD HOUSE PRESS

DEAR CAREGIVER, *The Decodables* series contains books following a systematic, cumulativ phonics scope and sequence aligned with the science of reading. Each book allows its reader to appl their phonics knowledge in engaging and relatable texts. The words within each text have been carefull selected to ensure that readers can rely on their decoding skills as they encounter new or unfamilia words. They also include high frequency words appropriate for the target skill level of the reader.

When reading these books with your child, encourage them to sound out words that are unfamiliar b attending to the target letter(s) and sounds. If the unknown word is an irregularly spelled high frequenc word or a word containing a pattern that has yet to be taught (challenge words) you may encourage you child to attend to the known parts of the word and provide the pronunciation of the unknown part(s Rereading the texts multiple times will allow your child the opportunity to build their reading fluency, skill necessary for proficient comprehension.

You can be confident you are providing your child with opportunities to build their decoding abilitie which will encourage their independence as they become lifelong readers.

Happy Reading!

Emily Nudds, M.S. Ed Literacy
Literacy Consultant

Norwood House Press • www.norwoodhousepress.com
The Decodables ©2024 by Norwood House Press. All Rights Reserved.
Printed in the United States of America.
367N–082023

Library of Congress Cataloging-in-Publication Data has been filed and is available at
https://lccn.loc.gov/2023010443

Literacy Consultant: Emily Nudds, M.S.Ed Literacy
Editorial and Production Development and Management: Focus Strategic Communications Inc.
Editors: Christine Gaba, Christi Davis-Martell
Photo Credits: Shutterstock: AnnaNel (p. 18), Anterovium (p. 12), BlueRingMedia (p. 19), Danie
Maguire (p. 17), Designua (p. 7), DrivingJack Photography (pp. 10–11), Elizaveta Elesina (p. 18)
EreborMountain (p. 9), Georgi Baird (p. 4), Gerry Bishop (p. 21), GraphicsRF.com (p. 13),
J. Warren's Studio (p. 21), Kenneth Keifer (p. 16), Krivosheev Vitaly (p. 5), Iaksena (p. 4),
Macrovector (covers), Malgorzata WI (p. 15), mapichai (p. 8), Olga Vasilek (p. 20), Onelia Pena
(p. 4), ParraSan (p. 19), Rejdan (p. 14), sportoakimirka (p. 6), Virrage Images (cover, p. 5).

Hardcover ISBN: 978-1-68450-688-0   Paperback ISBN: 978-1-68404-902-8
eBook ISBN: 978-1-68404-957-8

Contents

A Busy Day

Gardens are busy in daylight. Flies move high and low. Bees can be spied on fiery red flowers. The wind blows and dries the bright green leaves. Although plants are quietly soaking up the sunlight, they are hard at work too.

Gardens are filled with busy insects.

4

It seems quiet in the garden at night.

So, what happens in a garden at night? Most animals go to sleep. Do the plants lie down and rest too?

It can be calm at night.

Daytime in the Garden

Plants work hard in the daylight. They need sun, air, and water to grow. Soil that is high in **nutrients** helps, too. If the **temperature** is just right, plants can make their own food.

This plant is just beginning to grow.

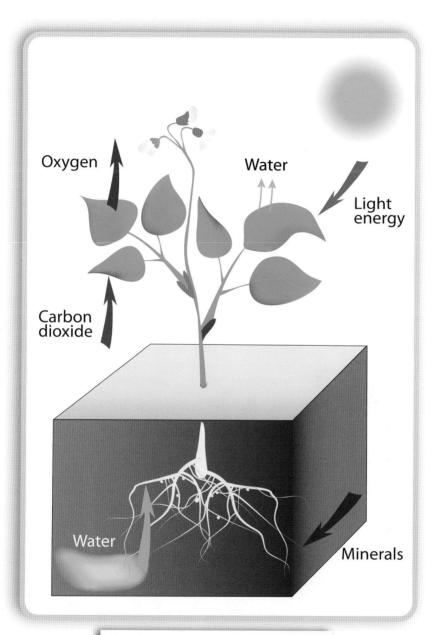

Oxygen

Water

Light energy

Carbon dioxide

Water

Minerals

The plant uses **energy** from the sunlight to help make food.

7

The leaf of the plant makes the food. It does the work through a process called **photosynthesis**. The plant uses light, water, and **carbon dioxide (CO$_2$)**.

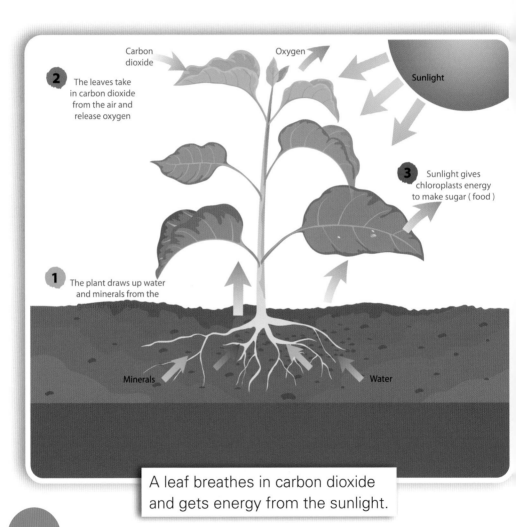

Carbon dioxide

Oxygen

Sunlight

2 The leaves take in carbon dioxide from the air and release oxygen

3 Sunlight gives chloroplasts energy to make sugar (food)

1 The plant draws up water and minerals from the

Minerals

Water

A leaf breathes in carbon dioxide and gets energy from the sunlight.

Many green plants have tiny holes called stomata in their leaves. One hole is called a stoma. The stomata open during the day to let air in. The leaf uses the carbon dioxide in the air during photosynthesis. The unneeded **oxygen (O_2)** in the air leaves the leaf through the stomata. Then they close at night when there is no photosynthesis to keep water from getting out. Each leaf has **chlorophyll**. Chlorophyll makes most leaves look a bright green.

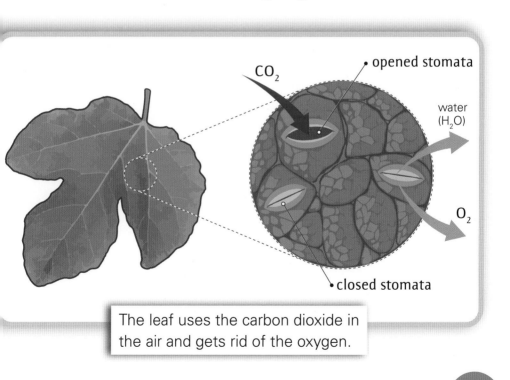

CO_2

opened stomata

water (H_2O)

O_2

closed stomata

The leaf uses the carbon dioxide in the air and gets rid of the oxygen.

Chlorophyll captures the sunlight. It uses the light energy to tie together water and carbon dioxide to make food. The plant uses some of the food. It stores the rest. The plant then breathes out oxygen. If there is no chlorophyll, the leaf will die.

Fall leaves are a beautiful sight.

In the fall, many leaves stop making food.
The chlorophyll stops and leaf colors change.
Forests can be alight with bright colors like
red, yellow, and orange.

11

Nighttime in the Garden

Plants follow a different pattern at night. Plants cannot make food at night. There is no sunlight. So instead, plants breathe, eat, and grow.

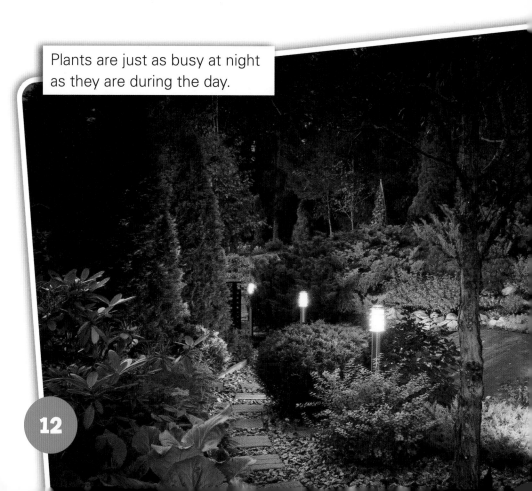

Plants are just as busy at night as they are during the day.

The plant uses the oxygen in the air at night. The oxygen mixes with the food that was made during the daylight. Then the plant enjoys a high-energy midnight snack.

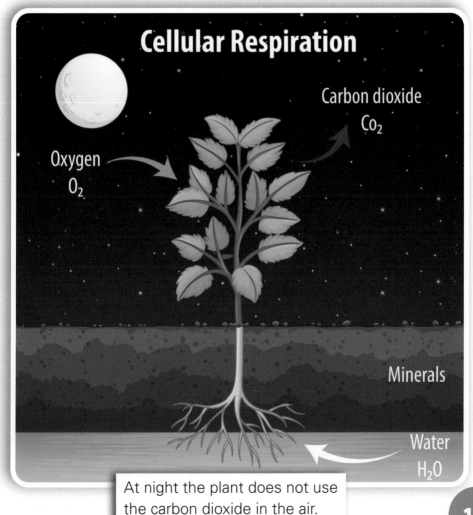

Cellular Respiration

Carbon dioxide
CO_2

Oxygen
O_2

Minerals

Water
H_2O

At night the plant does not use the carbon dioxide in the air.

A plant tries to use the food wisely. A plant might send the food to parts that are drier than others. It might feed its delightful flowers. It might fix a broken stem.

Some scientists think that some flowers close at night to keep the pollen from getting wet and heavy in the early morning dew.

Seedlings bend towards the sunlight.

Plants like light. They reach to the light so they can make more food. Trees in the rainforest grow very tall to reach the light. Little seedlings bend to find light. Plants in houses like to be in the window.

FUN FACT

Plants grow taller at night. This helps them reach more light during the day.

15

Nights in the Desert

In the desert, there is only a slight bit of rain. It is very hot and dry. The soil is often rocky or sandy.

In these hot places, plants fight to live. Their night pattern is different from other plants.

Cacti are a common sight in deserts.

Desert plants are not as green as plants that have lots of water.

In the desert, plant roots grow tight to the ground.

Desert plant leaves are tiny. They are not a very bright green.

Desert plants do not breathe during the day. They might lose too much water.

They breathe at night. The plant stores the carbon dioxide and waits for the morning sunlight to make food.

The leaves of desert plants are different from other leaves. Some are very thick. Cactus spines are really leaves!

Cactus spines are leaves that protect the cactus.

Some desert plants have thick leaves.

Pollination in the desert is different, too. Desert flowers bloom in the twilight. Less water is used at night. While some desert flowers are bright colors, many others are pale or white. These flowers do not depend on sight for pollination. They make a delightful smell. This brings insects and night-fliers to them.

Many insects like desert flowers.

The desert is busy at night.

19

FUN FACT

Moon gardens are gardens that have mostly white or silver plants. They are planted to be special in the light of the moon or at twilight. The pale flowers provide a silver light. They give off a delightful scent. Many people enjoy a moon garden in the twilight.

Moon gardens are a popular sight at night.

The Queen of the Night is a cactus that blooms one night each year. Its flower wilts before dawn.

A Queen of the Night cactus flower is a great highlight in the night.

The night may come, but plants are not allowed to rest. People and animals sleep, but plants have jobs to do all day and all night. They are busy doing jobs that help everyone.

A moon flower likes the night and the moonlight.

21

Glossary

carbon dioxide (CO_2) (kər-bĭn dī-ŏk-sīd): an invisible gas that is in the air; used by plants during photosynthesis

chlorophyll (klōr-ĕ-fĭl): a green material that makes leaves look green; it absorbs sunlight to help a plant make food

energy (ĕn-ər-jē): power to do work

nutrients (noo-trē-ənts): elements that are needed for healthy growth

oxygen (O_2) (ŏk-sĭ-jən): an invisible gas that is in the air; people must breathe it in to live

photosynthesis (fō-tō-sĭn-thə-sĭs): the process in which green plants use sunlight to make food

pollination (pŏl-ə-nā-shən): the transfer of pollen from flower to flower

temperature (tĕm-pər-ă-chər): the measure of hot and cold

Index

Vowel Teams

ie			igh				
die	flies	spied	alight	fight	light	right	slight
dries	lie		bright	high	night	sight	sunlight
			daylight	highlight			

High-Frequency Words

air	different	give	most	only	very
animals	does	great	move	through	work
before	follow	live	off	too	

Challenging Words

allowed	captures	fiery	food	leaves	quietly
busy	delightful	find	garden	parts	twilight
calm	desert	fliers	grow	process	window